DEC - - 2012

weeded

DATE DUE

PRINTED IN U.S.A.

Latino Folklore and Culture

Hispanic Americans: Major Minority

BOTH PUERTO RICAN AND AMERICAN

CENTRAL AMERICAN IMMIGRANTS

CUBAN AMERICANS

LATINO AMERICAN CIVIL RIGHTS

LATINO AMERICAN CUISINE

LATINO AMERICANS AND IMMIGRATION LAWS

LATINO AMERICANS AND RELIGION

LATINO AMERICANS AND THEIR JOBS

LATINO ARTS IN THE UNITED STATES

LATINO FOLKLORE AND CULTURE

LATINO MIGRANT WORKERS

LATINOS TODAY

MEXICAN AMERICANS

SOUTH AMERICAN IMMIGRANTS

SPAIN ARRIVES IN THE AMERICAS

TRAILBLAZING LATINO AMERICANS

Latino Folklore and Culture

Bill Palmer

Mason Crest

Mason Crest
370 Reed Road
Broomall, Pennsylvania 19008
www.masoncrest.com

Copyright © 2013 by Mason Crest, an imprint of National Highlights, Inc. All rights reserved. No part of this publication may be reproduced or transmitted in any form or by any means, electronic or mechanical, including photocopying, recording, taping, or any information storage and retrieval system, without permission from the publisher.

Printed and bound in the United States of America.

First printing
9 8 7 6 5 4 3 2 1

Library of Congress Cataloging-in-Publication Data

Palmer, Bill.
 Latino folklore and culture / Bill Palmer.
    p. cm.
 Includes index.
 ISBN 978-1-4222-2325-3 (hardcover) — ISBN 978-1-4222-2315-4 (hardcover series) — ISBN 978-1-4222-9329-4 (ebook)

 1. Hispanic Americans—Folklore. 2. Latin Americans—Folklore. 3. Hispanic Americans—Social life and customs. 4. Latin Americans—Social life and customs. I. Title.
 GR111.H57P35 2012
 398.208968073—dc22
                    2010051961

Produced by Harding House Publishing Service, Inc.
www.hardinghousepages.com
Interior design by Micaela Sanna.
Cover design by Torque Advertising + Design.
Printed in USA.

Contents

Introduction   6
1. Folklore and Culture   9
2. Old Stories   21
3. The Family   35
4. A World Full of Wonder   49
Time Line   59
Find Out More   60
Index   62
Picture Credits   63
About the Author and the Consultant   64

Introduction

by José E. Limón, Ph.D.

Even before there was a United States, Hispanics were present in what would become this country. Beginning in the sixteenth century, Spanish explorers traversed North America, and their explorations encouraged settlement as early as the sixteenth century in what is now northern New Mexico and Florida, and as late as the mid-eighteenth century in what is now southern Texas and California.

Later, in the nineteenth century, following Spain's gradual withdrawal from the New World, Mexico in particular established its own distinctive presence in what is now the southwestern part of the United States, a presence reinforced in the first half of the twentieth century by substantial immigration from that country. At the close of the nineteenth century, the U.S. war with Spain brought Cuba and Puerto Rico into an interactive relationship with the United States, the latter in a special political and economic affiliation with the United States even as American power influenced the course of almost every other Latin American country.

The books in this series remind us of these historical origins, even as each explores the present reality of different Hispanic groups. Some of these books explore the contemporary social origins—what social scientists call the "push" factors—behind the accelerating Hispanic immigration to America: political instability, economic underdevelopment and crisis, environmental degradation, impoverished or wholly absent educational systems, and other circumstances contribute to many Latin Americans deciding they will be better off in the United States.

And, for the most part, they will be. The vast majority come to work and work very hard, in order to earn better wages than they would back home. They fill significant labor needs in the U.S. economy and contribute to the economy through lower consumer prices and sales taxes.

When they leave their home countries, many immigrants may initially fear that they are leaving behind vital and important aspects of their home cultures: the Spanish language, kinship ties, food, music, folklore, and the arts. But as these books also make clear, culture is a fluid thing, and these native cultures are not only brought to America, they are also replenished in the United States in fascinating and novel ways. These books further suggest to us that Hispanic groups enhance American culture as a whole.

Our country—especially the young, future leaders who will read these books—can only benefit by the fair and full knowledge these authors provide about the socio-historical origins and contemporary cultural manifestations of America's Hispanic heritage.

chapter 1
Folklore and Culture

How are a ghost story, a wise saying, and a birthday party all alike?

They're all parts of folklore.

They're also parts of culture.

What Is Folklore?

"Folk" means ordinary people. "Lore" means knowledge. Knowledge can be shared in many ways. A story can pass along knowledge. A dance can pass along a different kind of knowledge. So can a holiday celebration. Even a riddle can tell you something important about the world. When you put the two words together—folk and lore—you get a word that has to do with all the ways ordinary people tell each other what they know about the world.

Folklore is not usually the kind of knowledge you learn in school. Instead, it might be the old stories grown-ups tell around the dinner table on holidays. It could be a bedtime story or a lullaby. It might be a story friends whisper to each other at a sleepover. It might be a dance or a kind of picture. It could even be a special meal.

Groups of people often have their own folklore. Sharing their stories, songs, crafts, and holidays ties people together. It helps link them to their past. It tells them how they are different from the rest of the world. It's a way to teach children who they are in the bigger world. Folklore helps people know who they are.

Folklore also helps us understand other groups of people better. Folklore can be a fun way to learn about other cultures.

What Is Culture?

Culture is a word people use to talk about a group of people. These people probably come from the same place. They probably speak the same language. They may believe the same things about God. They share lots of beliefs. They may eat the same foods. They do many things the same way.

In this book, we'll be talking about the folklore and culture of the Hispanic people in the United States. This group of people also calls themselves Latino. Latino folklore ties Hispanic Americans together. It gives them a sense of who they are. It helps them understand their culture. And we can understand their culture better by learning about Latino folklore, as well.

Nineteenth-century Latino folk art often portrayed Mary. Here her triangular skirt served as a reminder of the mountains, which figured in Native folk beliefs.

What Does It Mean to Be Latino or Hispanic? (And Is There a Difference?)

We've all heard the story of Christopher Columbus. More than five hundred years ago, in 1492, Columbus sailed across the Atlantic Ocean from Europe. Finally, he saw land. He thought he had landed in India. Really, though, he had landed in what Europeans would call the Americas.

> ## DID COLUMBUS DISCOVER AMERICA?
>
> People sometimes say that Columbus discovered America. But you can't really discover a place where millions of people already live! Europeans called America a New World—but for the Native people who already lived there, it was just the world.

The king and queen of Spain had paid for Columbus's journey. When Columbus found land, he claimed it for Spain. He didn't worry about the millions of people who already lived there. He said that the entire "New World" belonged to Spain!

For the next three hundred years, Spain said it owned much of what is now North, Central, and South America. Spain took the land that belonged to the **Native** people. Spanish soldier used guns to take the Natives' lands.

Spanish priests came to the Americas too. The priests taught the Natives about Christianity. They told them they must give up their old ways of praying and worshipping God.

> **Native** means the people who have lived in a place for a long time. It can also mean the culture of those people.

Folklore and Culture

Ruins left behind by the sophisticated Native cultures of the Western Hemisphere

More and more Spanish people came to the Americas. They built homes there. Some of the Spanish men married Native women. They had children who were part Spanish and part Native.

The Spanish brought with them slaves from Africa. These people also married the Native people in the New World. They had children too.

These new families learned from each other. They shared their cultures and their folklore. Together, they formed a brand-new culture. It was a mixture. Slowly, its own folklore grew. This folklore had little pieces of Spanish, Native, and African folklore. Their folklore was a mix, too.

Now the people in the Spanish **colonies** had their own stories. They made their own special foods. They sang their own songs. They prayed to God in their own ways. And most of them spoke Spanish.

In the 1980s, the U.S. government came up with the name "Hispanic" for this group of people. Not everyone likes this name. Many people don't like the way the term lumps everyone together based only

A street vendor sells Hispanic folk crafts.

> **Colonies** are places where people from another country have come to live and build a new home.

Folklore and Culture

13

A re-creation of a Spanish settler's home

WHAT IS LATIN AMERICA?

The Spanish-speaking countries in North and South America are called Latin America. They include:

- Mexico
- Guatemala
- El Salvador
- Honduras
- Nicaragua
- Costa Rica
- Panama
- Cuba
- Dominican Republic
- Venezuela
- Colombia
- Ecuador
- Peru
- Bolivia
- Paraguay
- Uruguay
- Argentina
- Chile
- Puerto Rico (part of the United States)
- Brazil

LATINO FOLKLORE AND CULTURE

on language. The people in North and South America who speak Spanish have a very different culture from Spain's. Other people use the word "Latino" for this same group of people. They like this word better because it has more to do with Latin America than with Spain.

The fact that Hispanics—or Latinos—don't agree on which term to use for themselves shows how **diverse** they are. They come from many different countries. They have different stories.

But at the same time, Hispanic American cultures have many things in common. They share many of the same

> Something that is **diverse** is made up of all kinds of different things.

Colorful Latino fabrics.

Folklore and Culture

WISE WORDS

Latino *dichos* (dee-choes) are proverbs (or wise sayings) that have been told for hundreds of years. No one remembers who the first person to say them was. They've been a part of Hispanic folklore for as long as anyone can remember. Some may have come from Spain. Others came from Native wise people. Others found their way here from Africa. Still others came from the Muslim world that once ruled Spain. These are very old words. They help us understand the deepest beliefs of the Hispanic people.

Here are a few examples:

Each person is a separate world.

Politeness is worth a great deal and costs little.

He who goes slowly goes far.

The person who does more than she can does more than she should.

Work makes a man stronger.

Charity begins with yourself.

stories. They often worship God the same way. Many of the same things are important to them. They are proud of their art and music. They celebrate the same holidays.

In the twenty-first century, Latinos have become the largest minority group in the United States. The number of Hispanic Americans nearly doubled between 1990 and 2004—from 22.4 million to almost 40 million people. That's almost two out of every ten Americans!

But the Latino culture has always been an important part of America. Until the 1800s, a lot of the West and Southwest was part of New Spain. Latinos helped build America, right from the very beginning.

Painted decorations in a New Mexican church, dating back to the 1700s, reveal the influence of Latino folk art.

 Today, Hispanic Americans are an even more important part of the United States. They help make America strong. And their folklore and culture help make the United States such an interesting place to live.

Folklore and Culture

LATINOS TODAY

In the twenty-first century, Latinos have become the largest minority group in the United States. (A minority is a group of people different from most of the other people in the country. Blacks, Asians, and Latinos are all minorities in the United States—but in a country like Kenya in Africa, for example, whites would be a minority.) In 2010, there were almost 50 million Hispanics (Latinos) in the United States. That's about 15 percent of America's total population—which means that if you had 100 Americans in a room, 15 of them would be likely to be

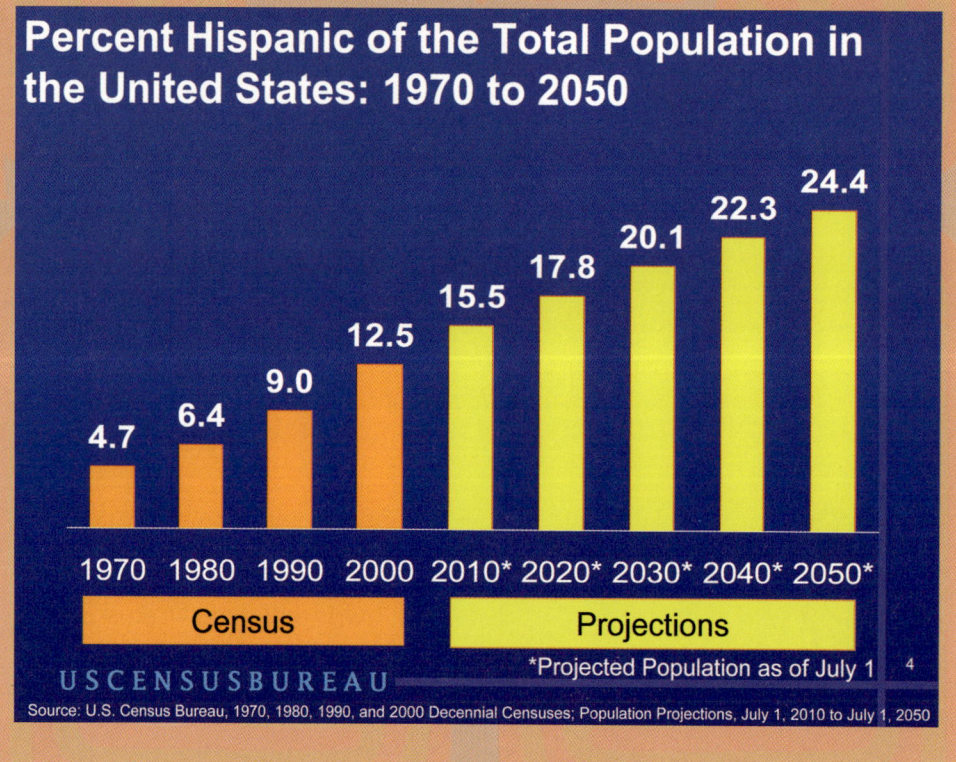

Hispanic Origin by Type: 2006

Type of origin	Number	Percent
Total	44,252,278	100.0
Mexican	28,339,354	64.0
Puerto Rican	3,987,947	9.0
Cuban	1,520,276	3.4
Dominican	1,217,225	2.8
Central American	3,372,090	7.6
South American	2,421,297	5.5
Other Hispanic	3,394,089	7.7

USCENSUSBUREAU
Source: U.S. Census Bureau, 2006 American Community Survey

Hispanics. Most Latinos, however, live in the western part of the United States, although more and more of them are moving to the East as well.

These Americans have roots in both Spain and the Americas. They have taken what's best from their past. They've added that to all the good things in the United States. They have faced a lot hardship along the way. They have had to fight for their rights. They are still fighting those battles. But Latinos today are becoming successful. They are doing a good job in every area of American life!

Folklore and Culture

chapter 2
Old Stories

Miguel and Maria Alvarez live in San Antonio, Texas. San Antonio is a city where Latino people have lived for more than 300 years! Miguel and Maria's parents speak both English and Spanish. Their grandmother speaks mostly Spanish. Miguel and Maria call their grandmother *abuelita*. That means "grandma" in Spanish.

Miguel and Maria love their abuelita very much. They go to her house every day after school. Abuelita is very proud of her Mexican culture. She teaches her grandchildren to be proud, too. She tells them wonderful stories. She sings songs in Spanish.

Miguel and Maria are **bilingual**. They can speak and understand both English and Spanish. They speak English at school. They speak Spanish with their abuelita. Spanish makes them feel close to her. Many of the people in Miguel and Maria's family are bilingual, too. Some of the older people speak mostly Spanish.

*Someone who is **bilingual** speaks two languages.*

One of the stories that their abuelita tells them is about the Crying Woman. It's a Latino ghost story that goes like this.

The Crying Woman

It was a dark night. Juan was coming home late after a long day at work. He was tired and hungry. The way to his house was very dark, and he walked faster. He just wanted to get home.

And then he saw something. A white shape moved toward him down the street. He blinked. He told himself it was mist. But the white shape

The Crying Woman is both an ancient folktale and modern urban lore.

LATINO FOLKLORE AND CULTURE

kept coming toward him. It looked like a woman.

The shape came closer. It was a beautiful woman. He could see her face now. He could hear her crying. She brushed past him. He felt her cold breath on his face. He heard her moan one last time. And then she was gone. The night was quiet again.

WHAT'S THE LESSON?

Read the Crying Woman story again. Can you think about what the lesson might be?

(Don't be out on the streets alone at night. It could be dangerous! Hurry home! That's a lesson that parents have been teaching children for a long time.)

Modern street graffiti portrays La Llorona's ghostly image. "La Llorona" is the Spanish way to say "Crying Woman."

Old Stories

Juan was shaking. He hurried into his house and shut the door behind him.

"What's the matter?" his wife asked him. "You look like you just saw a ghost."

"I did," Juan said. "I saw the Crying Woman."

Where Do Stories Come From?

Stories like the Crying Woman are part of Hispanic folklore. Many of these stories are very, very old. Sometimes they are stories about things

LATINO FOLKLORE AND CULTURE

THE GODDESS CIHUACOATL

According to long-ago Aztec stories, the goddess Cihuacoatl sometimes appeared on dark nights. She would be dressed in white robes that trailed behind her like a cloud. In the months before the white people came, the Aztecs said they heard Cihuacoatl moaning and sobbing. "Oh my children," she cried, "danger is coming. Run away! Oh my little ones, where will you be safe?"

Cihuacoatl was the Aztec goddess of the Earth, of war, and of birth. She carried a papoose on her back—but inside the cradle was a knife wrapped in a cloth. Her face was covered with white chalk. She wore a white dress. In some pictures, she looks pretty scary! The Aztecs believed that if you saw the goddess, it meant something bad was going to happen. At the same time, though, Cihuacoatl brought hope and new life with her.

Old Stories

that really happened in history. A lot of them are the **legends** of the Latino people. No one really knows who first told these stories. They have been told over and over for hundreds of years. They have been shared in families and in neighborhoods.

> **Legends** are made-up stories that have been told and retold for a long time.

Miguel and Maria learned the story of the Crying Woman from their abuelita. Their abuelita probably first heard the story when she was a child, too. Older people often tell folklore stories to younger people. The old stories are a way older people can teach young people lessons about life. Miguel and Maria's abuelita likes to tell her grandchildren old Mexican stories because she is proud of her Hispanic culture. Her grandchildren like the stories because they are fun to hear. They love to hear their grandmother speak Spanish

The Crying Woman's story unites the folklore of the "Old" and "New" Worlds.

LATINO FOLKLORE AND CULTURE

to them. They like the story of the Crying Woman because it is scary. But Latino parents and grandparents are teaching children a lesson, too, when they tell this story.

The Crying Woman is a very old story. Like the Latino people, it has its roots in both Spanish and Native cultures. The Spanish who came to the New World brought their old ghost stories with them. Some of these stories were about dead women who wandered the streets at night. The Native people of what we now call Mexico had their own scary stories. One of them was about a goddess named Cihuacoatl. She moaned through the towns at night looking for her lost children. The Spanish story mixed with the Native story, just like Native families mixed with Spanish families. The story of the Crying Woman came out of that mix of cultures. Many of the old stories Hispanic people tell mix Spanish and Native folklore.

An Old Story of Faith and Hope

On Sundays, Miguel and Maria's family goes to a beautiful church called Our Lady of Guadalupe. Our Lady of Guadalupe is very important to the Latino people. Her story is the one Hispanic Americans love best of all. It is a story about their faith in God. It is a story about the strength of the Latino people. They have been telling this story for almost 500 years! The story goes like this.

Juan Diego was a poor Native man. The Spanish had conquered his country. Many of his people had died in the war. Others had gotten sick and died. And now, the new Spanish rulers wanted the Native people to give up their old beliefs. The Spanish wanted the Natives to become Christians.

The Native people didn't want to give up their old ways. This was a time of great sadness in Mexico. The people were losing hope for their future. Juan Diego was sad and discouraged.

A street mural in Los Angeles reflects the Native traditions woven through the Virgin's story.

A modern street mural of the Virgin of Guadalupe.

On the morning of December 9, 1531, Juan Diego was walking in the hills outside Mexico City. Suddenly, he saw a beautiful woman. She glowed with light. Then she spoke to Juan Diego in his own language. She told him that she was Mary, the mother of Jesus. She told him she understood how hard things were for Juan and his people. She promised him she would always love and care for the people of Mexico. She would protect and watch over them. They would always have hope. She asked that a beautiful church be built on the spot Juan Diego saw her.

Juan Diego told his story to the Spanish priests. They did not believe him. But then a **miracle** took place! A picture of

> A **miracle** is when something really good happens that is very hard to explain.

Old Stories

An 18th-century painting of the Virgin of Guadalupe in a New Mexican church.

More than 35 million people in the United States speak Spanish with their families. That makes Spanish the second-most common language in the United States! (English is most common.) More Spanish-speaking people live in the United States than anywhere else in the world except Mexico. The Spanish language is one of the most important parts of Hispanic American culture. It is the language of home. It is the language of family and the neighborhood. It is a rich and beautiful language of songs and stories.

the lady he had seen was on the inside of his coat. When the priests saw it, they believed Juan Diego.

A great church was built on the hill where Mary had appeared to Juan Diego, at a place called Guadalupe. People from all over Mexico came to this church to pray together. Our Lady of Guadalupe brought them together. Now it didn't matter so much if they were Native or Spanish.

Our Lady of Guadalupe became a **symbol** of God's love and care for the people of Mexico and the New World. The Latino people love Our Lady of Guadalupe. They believe she has watched over them and loved them for hundreds of years. She is their mother. Millions of Hispanic people still visit her church every year. They look at her picture on Juan Diego's coat. This picture—a beautiful woman in blue that shines with light—is seen all over Mexico and wherever Latinos live. She is a symbol of the Latino people and their faith in God. Our Lady of Guadalupe is celebrated on December 12. It is a very special day for Latinos.

> A **symbol** *is something that people use to remind them of important ideas.*

Old Stories

A street shrine to the Virgin of Guadalupe is surrounded by the symbols of individuals' faith.

The story of the miracle of Our Lady of Guadalupe has roots in both Native and Spanish culture. In that way, it is like the story of the Crying Woman. One is an old ghost story. One is an old story of faith in God.

Hispanic people still share these stories and stories like them with each other. Older people pass them on to their children and grandchildren. They are an important part of Latino culture. These stories help Latino people understand who they are. They help them understand where they come from. They are a part of the pride and history of Hispanic Americans.

chapter 3
The Family

Diana Fernandez lives in New York City. She was born there. Her parents come from the Dominican Republic. Diana is in the fourth grade.

Diana has a big family. She is the youngest of five children. Her mother is one of nine children. Her father has twelve brothers and sisters. Most of Diana's aunts and uncles live in New York, too. They all have children and grandchildren. When Diana's whole family gets together, there are

> The Dominican Republic is a country in the Caribbean Sea. It shares the same island with the country of Haiti. It is the place where Christopher Columbus first landed in 1492. It was the first colony of Spain in the New World. Some of the very first Latino families, part Spanish and part Native, lived here. Today around ten million people live in the Dominican Republic. Many people visit to enjoy its warm weather and beautiful beaches. The capital and largest city is called Santo Domingo. Sugar cane is the number one crop grown in the Dominican Republic. Baseball is very popular and some of the greatest players in the world are Dominican. Over a million people in the United States belong to families that come from the Dominican Republic.

First Holy Communion is an important event in the lives of many Latino Americans.

more than a hundred people! Her father likes to say they are a REAL Dominican family. Their family is big, happy, and strong.

Diana had her First Holy Communion in May. It was one of the happiest days of her life. She wore a beautiful white dress. She felt very close to God that day.

After they went to church, her family had a big party for her. Her parent's apartment was too small for all the guests, so the party was at her Aunt Rosa's house in New Jersey. There were tables under a big tent. There were plates of delicious food. Her Uncle Hector cooked a whole pig in a pit in the ground. He did it just the way he used to do it in the Dominican Republic. There was music and laughter and fun. There were old people, young people, kids, and babies. Diana met three new cousins

LATINO FOLKLORE AND CULTURE

who had just come to New York from Santo Domingo. She found out she had an uncle who played first base for the Chicago Cubs. The adults talked and laughed. The kids played tag. Everyone had a good time.

In the car on the way home, Diana smiled to herself. Her First Communion had been the best day of her life. Her family had helped make it special. "*Mi familia,*" she whispered to herself. "My family."

The First Hispanic Family

The story of the Hispanic people begins as a story of a family. Soon after the Spanish came to the New World in 1492, the first Latina (or Latino) baby was born in America. That baby had a Spanish father and a Native mother. The baby was the start of a whole new culture. This new culture was a mix of Spanish and Native cultures.

Latinos sometimes call this *la raza*, the people. Latinos celebrate October 12—the day America calls Columbus Day—as *La Día de la Raza*, the Day of the People. This day helps Hispanic Americans remember that first Latino family. It makes them feel proud.

For over five hundred years, the family has been a very important part of Hispanic culture. Every family is different. But Latino families are alike too.

This street mural portrays the birth of "La Raza," the first Latinos.

The Family

A Latino Folktale

There was once a rich man who had four sons—Pedro, Diego, José, and Manuel. The brothers had everything they needed. But they always wanted just a little bit more. So one day, the brothers decided to look for new riches. Even their littlest brother, Manuel, would come with them. Like all Latino men, he was as brave and manly as his older brothers.

The four brothers had not gone far, when they stopped. The road went in four separate directions. "Which way shall we go?" Manuel asked.

Pedro, the oldest, told each of the brothers to take a different road. "We'll each seek our fortune. After one year, we will meet here again." So each brother set out on his own path.

Pedro came to the house of a thief. The man taught Pedro how to steal. "No thief is as good as me," the man bragged. "I have never been caught." Soon, Pedro knew three times what the thief did. Pedro was so smooth he could take money right from under your nose!

Meanwhile, Diego was staying with a great hunter. Diego learned how to hunt. He didn't even have to look when he aimed his gun.

Things were going well for José too. He was staying with a doctor. Soon, José could heal anyone who was sick. He was especially good at setting bones.

And little Manuel ended up at the house of a fortune-teller. He learned to "see" what his father and each of his brothers were doing.

After a year, Manuel packed up a suitcase full of gold he had earned. He hurried to meet his brothers. They each had a suitcase of their own. The suitcases were nearly bursting with coins. They went home happy to their father.

Then a rich man who lived nearby sent a message to the four brothers. His daughter was lost. He wanted the four brothers to help him find her.

Some see true machismo as being shown by Latino men who protect their children and provide them with strong role models.

"As soon as you bring her home," he said, "the one who works the hardest shall be her husband."

The four brothers found out that a giant named Old Long Arms had taken the girl. Young Manuel had a plan. "Pedro, you be the one who steals the princess. I'll tell you where she is hidden. And Diego can take a shot at the giant if need be."

The plan went well. The brothers escaped with the girl by boat. But Old Long Arms followed them. Quick as a flash, Diego shot the giant. The

The Family

giant crashed into their boat. The wood broke and the water rushed in. José realized that wood is not so different from bone. He put the boat back together again. They went safely home.

When the girl's father saw her, he was so happy he jumped up and down. "Which of these young men worked the hardest?" he asked.

The girl told him what had happened. Her father scratched his head. They had all worked hard.

"She's mine, she's mine!" the four brothers each shouted.

The girl's father laughed. "Don't be silly! I have four daughters—one for each of you."

And so the four brothers married. They lived happily ever after. And they got richer every year.

The four brothers are "typical" Latino men. They're brave, strong, and willing to fight. They are winners every time. In today's world, not everyone agrees that this is a good way to be. Many Latinos no longer think men should act like this. They think men and women should be equal.

Modern Latino Families

A Latino man is supposed to be "macho." This means he is strong, hard working, and tough. Many Latino fathers are strict with their children. They expect to make all the rules in the family.

Women are supposed to be strong, too. They take care of the children and the home. They cook the family's meals. They go to church and teach the children about religion. They obey and respect their husbands.

Children are taught to love and respect their parents. Hispanic children learn to respect all people who are older than them. They know they are expected to love each other. They learn to be loyal to each other. They look out for each other. They take care of each other no matter what happens.

Each family has its own stories, history, and folklore. The family celebrates happy times and holidays together. It shares the hard times, too. The family makes each other strong. Family is very important to Latinos.

Holidays and Family Celebrations

Many Hispanic families are Roman Catholic. The Spanish taught the Catholic religion to the Native people. The Catholic religion celebrates many special days. Latino families celebrate these at church. Then they have big family meals at home. Baptisms, First Communions, Confirmations, weddings, and funerals bring Latino families together. On November 2nd, many Latinos celebrate the Day of the Dead. They remember their relatives who have died. There are parades, church services, a visit to a cemetery, and family feasts with special holiday food. It is a fun

Leona Medina-Tiede, owner of a restaurant in Chimayo, New Mexico, with her grandchildren.

The Family

Day of the Dead cut-paper art.

festival that's a little sad, too.

Many Hispanic girls have a quinceañera. This is a big, big party for her fifteenth birthday. It's the day she becomes a young woman. She wears a beautiful dress. All her friends and family come to dance and eat together. Her parents show the world how proud they are of their daughter!

Hispanic families celebrate together in many different ways. Food is almost always a big part of any family celebration. Often the special meals come from old family recipes. Food can be a kind of folklore, too! And folklore is shared around the table. The older people share memories of what life was like when they were young. Families get to know one another better. Cousins meet cousins and become friends. Family celebrations are fun! They help make families strong. They're a time for families to take pride in who they are and where they come from.

The Quinceañera

"It's perfect," says Mia Duarte. She watches her big sister Teresa put on the beautiful white dress. "It's the prettiest thing I've ever seen."

LATINO FOLKLORE AND CULTURE

Teresa is getting ready for her quinceañera. That's a big party Latino families have on girls' fifteenth birthdays.

Mia and Teresa's parents have eight older children. Teresa is the first in the family to have a quinceañera. The party will cost as much as a wedding. Until now, the Duartes didn't have enough money.

Seven years ago, the Duarte family left Mexico. They moved to California. Then they moved to Kentucky. Mia doesn't remember much about Mexico. She dreams about it, though. She thinks it must be a wonderful place. But she's glad she lives in the United States. She's glad her family has more money they did in Mexico.

A quinceañera is a big event in the life of a Latina girl!

The Family

Mia and Teresa's older brothers and sisters had to drop out of school. The family needed them to go to work. Teresa will be the first to finish high school. Mia is very proud of her sister.

All the plans for Teresa's quinceañera took a full year. Relatives around the country sent money to help with the cost. Family all the way from California are coming to the party.

Mia smiles at her sister. She can't wait till it's her turn to have a quinceañera!

Who's Part of a Latino Family?

When many Americans think of family, they think of what is called a **nuclear** family. A nuclear family is made up of parents and their children who live together. Nowadays, many American families are even smaller. Many families have only one parent instead of two.

Most Hispanic American families are much bigger. They are made up of several **generations** of family members. Grandparents, aunts and uncles, and cousins may live near each other. Sometimes they even share the same house. They see each other a lot. They do many things together as a family.

> **Nuclear** means a family that is made up of a father, a mother, and their children.

Grandparents are very important members of the Latino family. In the United States, many Hispanic mothers work outside the home. Grandparents often care for their young grandchildren during the day. Grandparents and grandchildren are very close.

Aunts, uncles, and godparents are also important parts of the family. Children in Latino families get to know their relatives very well. Most Hispanic kids have many cousins around their own age. They often become good friends for life.

Families in all cultures love their children, but Latinos do so especially. Many American families consider it the parents' responsibility to raise the children, but Latinos expect everyone—grandparents, aunts, uncles, godparents—to teach and care for children. Home is often a warm and loving place. In many Latino households, grown children stay home until they are married.

Children treat the elders in their families with respect and honor. This means they obey their parents, grandparents,

> **Generations** *are groups of people of the same age in a family. You, your parents, and your grandparents make up three different generations.*

Grandparents are a very important part of Latino extended families.

The Family 45

The future lies with young Latino families like this one.

and aunts and uncles. Arguing is usually not allowed! But children know they can always trust the older people in their family. A Latino young person always has family members who will help and support them as they grow up.

Strength and Support

A strong family has helped Hispanic Americans get along. If they come from a different country, this is especially important. The family helps them face hard times together. It helps them learn about who they are. And it's fun!

LATINO FOLKLORE AND CULTURE

The family prays together. They eat delicious food together. They share their folklore and culture. They speak the Spanish language together. Like any family, Latino families are not perfect. But the love and respect they show for one another is a wonderful thing. The family gives meaning to life. It is a great strength and pride of the Latino people.

chapter 4
A World Full of Wonder

Rafa Fuentes watched candlelight flicker over his family's faces. Everyone he loved was here with him. His mother and father, his two little sisters, and his grandfather were all here.

But other people were here, too, people Rafa couldn't see. His grandma who died last winter, his brother who died when Rafa was still a baby, and

A Day of the Dead altar

Another Day of the Dead altar

his other grandparents, who had gone to heaven before Rafa was born. Rafa knew they were all here. And there were other guests in the room, people so familiar they seemed like part of the Fuentes family. People like César Chávez, the Latino leader, and Selena, the beautiful singer who died the year Rafa was born. The small room was alive with souls. Rafa thought he could almost see them in the candlelight from each *ofrenda*.

The ofrendas were **altars**. They were little tables Rafa and his sisters had helped decorate. Pretty colored paper hung from the ceiling over each altar. The dead person's favorite things were on each table. One table held their brother's favorite toy and the little cup he had used. Another held their grandparents' books. The newest ofrenda had Grandma's knitting needles and her favorite blue sweater. Each little table had a photo of the person. Rafa and his sisters had made drawings for their

Altars *are tables where special religious things are kept and shown.*

LATINO FOLKLORE AND CULTURE

For weeks before the Day of the Dead, the markets of Mexico and the Latino communities in the Southwest United States, are filled with skeletons! Made of wood, plastic, metal (and sometimes candy!) these miniature skeletons are shown doing all the kinds of things living people do: skeletons at work, skeletons eating and drinking, skeletons dancing, even dog skeletons chasing cat skeletons. Latino people use these skeleton figures as decorations around their homes and on their family *ofrendas*. The skeletons look funny doing the things living people do, and they are partly meant as a joke. But they remind people that maybe the living and the dead are not really all that different!

Day of the Dead cookies

A World Full of Wonder

brother. These were on his ofrenda, too. They had written notes to their grandma. Their mother had made special foods for her parents.

She had also made *pan de muerto*—the sweet bread for the dead. She had bought sugar skulls for the children. Rafa and his sisters put bouquets of marigolds on every altar. They hung paper skeletons from all the doorways.

Rafa looked up at his favorite skeleton. The skeleton seemed to wink and grin back at him. Rafa smiled. He remembered how sad he had been when his grandma died. Now he no longer felt so bad. Grandma

Pan de Muerto

LATINO FOLKLORE AND CULTURE

was right here in the room with them. He couldn't see her, but he believed she was there. The skeleton's grin made him feel better. He could almost hear his grandma laugh.

An Ancient Tradition

Long ago, the Native people of Mexico and other countries in Central America believed that once a year the souls of the dead could come back to the world of the living. The Natives believed the world of the living and the world of the dead were both real. During that special time, the dead could visit their families and enjoy themselves. They could eat the foods they loved when they were alive. They could be together with the people they loved. It was a happy time for both the living and the dead. This special time lasted a whole month. It was a time to laugh and eat. Skulls smiled down at everyone. The skull reminded people that death was not the end of life.

A Day of the Dead procession

When the Spanish arrived, people had been celebrating like this for more than three thousand years. The Spanish thought death was serious and very scary. They did not understand the Native people's way of honoring the dead with a happy celebration. The Spanish Catholic priests wanted to **convert** the Native people to the Christian religion. They tried to stop them from celebrating their festival of the dead.

> To **convert** means to change from one religion to another.

But the Native people would not let go of their beliefs. They were too important to them. Finally, the Catholic priests decided to combine the Native festival with a Christian holy day. They moved the Day of the Dead to November 2, All Soul's Day. This was the day the Church remembered the Christian dead.

Día de Los Muertos (Day of the Dead) is still an important holiday for Latinos. Many people in Latin America and the United States celebrate with parades and parties. It is a day with lots of fun and music. It is also

Each straw cross woven into the fence represents a prayer put here by people visiting the church at Chimayó in New Mexico.

LATINO FOLKLORE AND CULTURE

a day when people remember their loved ones who have died. The Day of the Dead is both fun and serious. It is a day to celebrate the good things in life along with the love and memories of people who have died. It is a very special day for many Latinos.

Celebrating the Day of the Dead has become popular with many Americans who are not Hispanic. It is one of the many gifts Latinos have shared with all Americans. And like the Latino people themselves, the folklore behind the Day of the Dead is a mix of Native and Spanish culture.

Magic and Mystery

The faith and beliefs Latinos celebrate on the Day of the Dead are important to them all year. Many Hispanic Americans believe in the **supernatural** world. Their strong Christian faith and their old Native beliefs come together in the way they see the world.

Even the most ordinary day can be filled with magic and mystery. A woman might see a message from her dead husband written in soapsuds in her kitchen sink. A man driving home from work might feel Saint Barbara push on his foot. Then he stops the car in time to avoid an accident. A child who runs in front of traffic feels the strong hands of an angel pull her to safety. Most Latinos believe that these kinds of things are very real. They think things like this happen all the time.

> **Supernatural** *has to do with invisible powers, magic, and miracles.*

Faith in God and the invisible world is an important part of many Latinos' lives. They believe God runs the world in strange and wonderful ways. They believe God can make miracles happen!

Miracles can happen to people when they're all alone. Sometimes, they happen to whole groups of people. Some churches in the Southwest have a long history of miracles.

A World Full of Wonder

El Santuario de Chimayó

The Church of Chimayó

Nearly 200 years ago, in the small village of Chimayó in New Mexico, a miracle happened. A man was praying when he saw bright light shining from a hillside. He was amazed and excited. He began to dig into the hill. Buried in the earth was a crucifix, a small statue of Jesus on the cross.

A priest brought the crucifix to the city. Then it disappeared. It turned up back in its hole in Chimayó. This happened three times. Everyone understood now that the crucifix wanted to stay in Chimayó. A small church was built there. People came from all over to see the mysterious image of Jesus. Those who were sick got better. Those who were sad found joy. So many miracles happened that more and more people came to the tiny church.

Hispanic Americans believe the church is built on a very holy spot. They believe the soil there can heal the sick. The crucifix that started it all is still in the church. Each year during Holy Week (the week before Easter), thousands of people come to Chimayó to visit the church. They take away a little of the holy dirt. Many believe their prayers are answered here.

A Sense of Wonder

Some people might say that Latinos are **superstitious**. They see and believe in things they can't see. They can't prove these things are real. But their beliefs are very real and special to them. These beliefs help them understand life. They help make Hispanic Americans strong.

The Latino people believe life is full of surprises. They believe even sad times can be beautiful. These beliefs help them face life's hard times. Their beliefs give them many reasons to celebrate. Faith in a world of

> Someone who is **superstitious** believes in the supernatural, especially in good and bad luck.

A World Full of Wonder

The sky over New Mexico; Hispanic Americans believe life is lit with a deeper meaning.

magic and miracles brings Latinos together. Their strong faith is something all Americans can admire and appreciate.

Hispanic folklore and culture came from many parts of the world. The Native peoples of America, the people of Europe, and the people of Africa all helped make this special culture. It is richer and stronger because of this mix. No wonder Latinos are proud of who they are! They help make America stronger, too.

Time Line

1400s — The Spanish become the first Europeans to come to the Americas.

1492 — The first Europeans encounter the Native Indian world of the Americas, thus giving birth to the Hispanic culture.

1517 — Cortés arrives on the Yucatan Peninsula.

1531 — Our Lady the Virgin of Guadalupe appears to Juan Diego.

1824 — María Mercedes Barbudo is jailed in Puerto Rico for conspiring against the Spanish.

1840s — Feminism sweeps across North America.

1896 — The Shadow of the Cross painted by Henri Ault.

1960s — A second wave of feminism covers North America.

1980s — The U.S. government introduces the term "Hispanic."

Jan 2003 — The U.S. Census Bureau announces that Hispanics have become the country's largest minority group.

Find Out More

IN BOOKS

Ada, Alma Flor. *Pio Peep! Traditional Spanish Nursery Rhymes*. New York, N.Y.: Harper Collins Rayo, 2004.

Anzaldua, Gloria. *Prietita and the Ghost Woman*. San Francisco, Calif.: Children's Book Press, 2001.

Gerson, Mary-Joan. *Fiesta Femenina: Celebrating Women in Mexican Folktales*. New York, N.Y.: Barefoot Books, 2001.

Gonzalez, Ralfka. *My First Book of Proverbs/Mi Primer Libro de Dichos*. San Francisco, Calif.: Children's Book Press, 2002.

Lowery, Linda. *Day of the Dead*. Minneapolis, Minn.: Carolrhoda Books, 2004.

Winchester, Faith. *Hispanic Holidays.* Mankato, Minn.: Capstone Press, 2005.

ON THE INTERNET

Day of the Dead
www.azcentral.com/ent/dead

Day of the Dead in Mexico
www.dayofthedead.com

Hispanic Culture
www.hispanic-culture-online.com

Latino Folklore
www.americanfolklore.net/folklore/mexican-folklore/

Our Lady of Guadalupe
www.catholic.org/about/guadalupe.php

The Crying Woman
www.legendsofamerica.com/gh-lallorona.html

Index

Aztec 25

bilingual 21

Chávez, César 50
Chimayó 41, 56, 57
Christianity 11, 27, 54, 55
Cihuacoatl 25, 27
colonies 13, 35
Columbus, Christopher 11, 35, 37
Crying Woman, the 21–24, 26, 27, 33
culture 9–13, 15, 17, 21, 26, 27, 31, 33, 37, 45, 47, 50, 55, 58

Day of the Dead (Día de Los Muertos) 41, 42, 49, 51, 54, 55

First Holy Communion 36
folk art 10, 17

holiday 9, 17, 41, 54

La Llorona 23, 26
"La Raza" 37

Mary 10, 29, 31
minority 17, 18
miracle 29, 31, 55, 57, 58

"New World" 11, 13, 26, 27, 31, 35, 37

ofrendas 50, 51
Our Lady of Guadalupe (Virgin of Guadalupe) 27, 29–32, 59

pan de muerto 52

quinceañera 42–44

religion 40, 41, 54

slaves 13

Picture Credits

Andriy Petrenko | Dreamstime.com: p. 39

Benjamin Stewart: p. 32, 41, 46, 54, 56, 58

Corel: p. 15

Darla Hallmark | Dreamstime.com: p. 51

Imageexpress.com: p. 13

Jason Stitt | Dreamstime.com: p. 43

Jose Gil | Dreamstime.com: p. 53

Michelle Bouch: p. 22, 24, 25, 26, 42

Monkey Business Images | Dreamstime.com: p. 45

Photos.com: p. 23

Richard Gunion | Dreamstime.com: p. 36

Santuario de Chimayó, photographer Benjamin Stewart: p. 17, 20, 28, 30, 34, 48

Sarah Elizabeth Garland: p. 49, 52

Museum of Spanish Colonial Art, Santa Fe, N.M., photographer Benjamin Stewart: p. 10, 16

About the Author and the Consultant

Bill Palmer has been an editor and author for over twenty years. He studied anthropology in college and has a great interest in folklore and cultures from around the world. He thinks he may have the largest collection of Day of the Dead skeletons in the Upstate New York town where he lives.

Dr. José E. Limón is professor of Mexican-American Studies at the University of Texas at Austin where he has taught for twenty-five years. He has authored over forty articles and three books on Latino cultural studies and history. He lectures widely to academic audiences, civic groups, and K–12 educators.